HILLARY RODHAM
CLINTON
FIRST LADY AND SENATOR

SPECIAL LIVES IN HISTORY THAT BECOME

Signature LIVES

HILLARY RODHAM
CLINTON
FIRST LADY AND SENATOR

by Michael Burgan

Content Adviser: Sarah E. Brewer, Ph.D.,
Associate Director, Women and Politics Institute,
American University

Reading Adviser: Rosemary G. Palmer, Ph.D.,
Department of Literacy, College of Education,
Boise State University

Compass Point Books ◆ Minneapolis, Minnesota

Compass Point Books
3109 West 50th Street, #115
Minneapolis, MN 55410

This book was manufactured with paper containing at least
10 percent post-consumer waste.

Editor: Jennifer VanVoorst
Page Production: Heather Griffin and Bobbie Nuytten
Photo Researchers: Marcie C. Spence and Svetlana Zhurkin
Cartographer: XNR Productions, Inc.
Library Consultant: Kathleen Baxter

Creative Director: Keith Griffin
Editorial Director: Nick Healy
Managing Editor: Catherine Neitge

Library of Congress Cataloging-in-Publication Data
Burgan, Michael.
  Hillary Rodham Clinton : first lady and senator / by Michael Burgan.
      p. cm. — (Signature lives)
  Includes bibliographical references and index.
  ISBN 0-7565-1588-2 (hardcover)
  1. Clinton, Hillary Rodham—Juvenile literature. 2. Presidents'
spouses—United States—Biography—Juvenile literature.
3. Legislators—United States—Biography—Juvenile literature.
4. United States. Congress. Senate—Biography—Juvenile literature.
I. Title. II. Series.
  E887.C55B868 2008
  328.73092—dc22
  [B]   2005025209

Visit Compass Point Books on the Internet at *www.compasspointbooks.com*
or e-mail your request to *custserv@compasspointbooks.com*

Signature Lives

MODERN AMERICA

Life in the United States since the late 19th century
has undergone incredible changes. Advancements in
technology and in society itself have transformed the
lives of Americans. As they adjusted to this modern era,
people cast aside old ways and embraced new ideas. The
once silenced members of society—women, minorities,
and young people—made their voices heard. Modern
Americans survived wars, economic depression, protests,
and scandals to emerge strong and ready to face whatever
the future holds.

Table of Contents

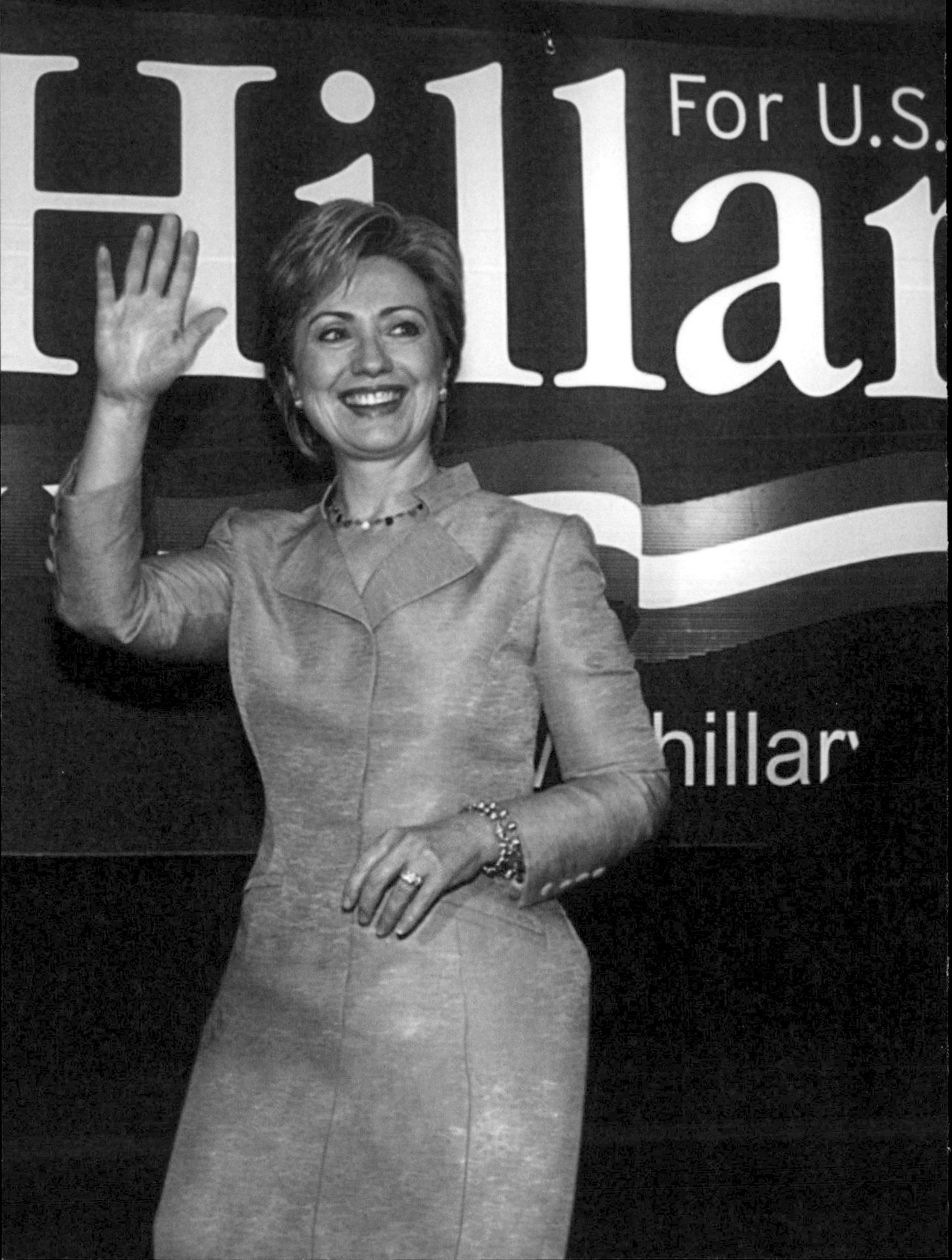

Hillar
For U.S.
hillar

Chapter

1

FIRST LADY
OF THE SENATE

ᔥᕔᕽᕒᕢ

Hillary Rodham Clinton looked out over the crowd gathered in the gym at the State University of New York in Purchase. It was February 6, 2000, and nearly 2,000 people had crowded into the building to hear her make a historic announcement. For the first time ever, the wife of a U.S. president was going to run for a national political office.

With President Bill Clinton, her daughter, Chelsea, and her mother by her side, Clinton told the crowd, "I am honored today to announce my candidacy to the United States Senate from New York." The first lady explained what she hoped to accomplish as a U.S. senator. She wanted to improve health care and education while creating new jobs. She said the government had an important role to

Hillary Rodham Clinton waved to reporters at a press conference following her historic victory in 2000 as the first spouse of a U.S. president to be elected to public office.

play in these and other issues, but she realized it could not solve every problem. She also recognized that her campaign for the Senate seat would not be easy.

Though Clinton had never before held elected office, she was no stranger to the political process. Her husband, Bill Clinton, was about to finish the second of two terms as president of the United States. The eight years of his presidency had been an exciting but difficult time for the Clintons. Even before Bill Clinton was elected president in 1992, news reporters examined his and his wife's private relationship. Once he won the presidency, reporters focused more attention on her than any other first lady before her. She endured her fair share of personal and political attacks.

But she soon proved herself to be an able politician in her own right. Many women admired her talents and her willingness to speak out on issues affecting women. They thought she successfully balanced being a wife and mother with having her own career outside the home. As if she were a rock star or a top athlete, Hillary Rodham Clinton was soon known by just her first name.

Not all Americans, however, liked Clinton or the role she played in the White House. To many conservatives, she represented a political threat. They opposed women who held feminist beliefs.

Clinton also often advised her husband on what to do, and some people were uncomfortable with a first lady playing such an influential role in policy.

Despite the attacks on her and her husband, Clinton wanted to serve the people of the United

Hillary Rodham Clinton played an active role during her husband's presidency, often accompanying him on international trips.

States—not as first lady, but as an elected official in her own right. With her announcement on February 6, 2000, she took the first step toward becoming Senator Hillary Rodham Clinton.

After an active campaign, first against New York City Mayor Rudy Giuliani and then against U.S. Representative Rick Lazio, Election Day finally arrived. On November 7, 2000, Clinton voted in her new hometown of Chappaqua, New York. She later wrote, "After seeing Bill's name on ballots for many years, I was thrilled and honored to see my own." The rest of New York's voters made their choice, too. What had once been a close race turned into an easy victory, as Clinton beat Lazio by nearly 800,000 votes. The first lady was about to become a U.S. senator. In this new role, she would have another chance to serve her country and its people.

The years since Clinton's historic election have been busy and fruitful. She has traveled around the country and internationally to discuss the nation's issues, including education, health care, and the war on terror. She was re-elected to the Senate in 2006, and in 2007, she announced

her desire to return to the White House—this time as president. Whatever the future holds, Hillary Rodham Clinton has left her mark as one of the most powerful and influential female political figures in United States history. ❧

Hillary Rodham Clinton met with Afghanistan's President Hamid Karzai during his official visit in January 2007.

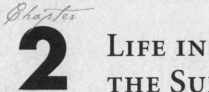

2 LIFE IN THE SUBURBS

❧∾❧

In 1945, the United States emerged from World War II as the richest and most powerful country in the world. Men and women returning from military duty began to start families and look for jobs. Hugh Rodham was one of those veterans. He had grown up in Pennsylvania and had become a salesman before the war. People who knew him said Rodham was perfect for his job—he loved to talk and could persuade anyone to buy almost anything.

Rodham's work took him to Chicago, Illinois, where he met Dorothy Howell. They married in 1942, just before Rodham entered the Navy. After the war, he worked in Chicago for a fabric company. On October 26, 1947, the Rodhams welcomed their first child—a baby girl they named Hillary Diane.

Hillary Rodham at Wellesley College in 1969

Less than three years later, the Rodhams had a son, named for his father. The Rodhams decided it was time to move out of the city and into a bigger home. Young Hillary spent most of her childhood in Park Ridge, Illinois, just outside Chicago.

During the 1950s, Park Ridge was swarming with kids—nearly 50 lived on the Rodhams' block alone. Dorothy Rodham stayed home to raise her children, which soon included another son, Tony. Meanwhile, Hugh Rodham drove every day to his job in Chicago. In 1956, he started a company that made drapes. He did fairly well with his business, but he hated

The Rodhams lived in a spacious home in the Chicago, Illinois, suburb of Park Ridge.

to spend money. He sometimes ignored his kids' requests for new clothes or their pleas to turn up the heat on winter nights so they would not be cold in the morning.

As a child, Hillary enjoyed playing basketball, softball, and other sports with the neighborhood children. For vacations, she and her family stayed at the Rodham family cabin in Pennsylvania's Pocono Mountains. There Hugh Rodman and his children fished, and Hillary learned how to shoot a gun, firing at tin cans.

Hillary also learned the importance of standing up for herself. When she was 4, a neighborhood girl named Suzy started pushing her around. Hillary told her mother she was afraid of the girl. Mrs. Rodham told her to challenge the bully. Hillary did and returned from the encounter exclaiming, "I can play with the boys now! And Suzy will be my friend!" She later wrote about this experience, saying her parents wanted her and her brothers "to be tough in order to survive what life

Hillary Rodham Clinton was one of roughly 76 million Americans born between 1946 and 1964—the so-called baby boom generation. Many soldiers who fought in World War II returned home and started families. Government aid helped these veterans go to college so they could find good jobs to support their new families. The aid also helped many veterans buy homes in the suburbs. The baby boomers grew up during a time when the U.S. economy also boomed. Later they would challenge many traditional American ideas about government and society.

may throw at us. They expected us to stand up for ourselves."

As she grew older, Hillary joined the Brownies and Girl Scouts. She won badges for holding bake sales, collecting food, and raising money for charities. Her greatest accomplishments, however, came at school. She was extremely smart and often brought home straight-A report cards. She believed that with hard work, she could reach any goal she set for herself, in or out of school. That belief, however, was crushed while she was in high school. Hillary wrote to the National Aeronautics and Space Administration to volunteer for astronaut training. She was outraged to learn that the agency had no plans to train female astronauts. She couldn't believe she could be kept from attaining her goals by the mere fact of her gender.

During high school, Hillary found time for activities outside the classroom. She played field hockey and enjoyed music. She and her friends gathered around a TV in February 1964 to watch the Beatles, a famous rock group, and the next year she attended a rock concert when the Rolling Stones played in Chicago.

Hillary showed an interest in politics at an early age, and she enjoyed talking about current events. A classmate recalled that in elementary school, he and Hillary discussed "lots of things that you wouldn't

*Hillary Rodham
(standing)
posed with
classmates from
Park Ridge in a
1964 yearbook
photo.*

expect fourth or fifth graders to think about." In high
school, Hillary won a seat on the student council and
was elected vice president of her junior class. She
also belonged to the Young Republicans and held
many conservative views.

Hugh Rodham was a dedicated Republican, like
most of the residents in Park Ridge. Republicans

The 1960 election featured Vice President Richard Nixon, a Republican, against Senator John F. Kennedy, a Democrat from Massachusetts. The race was close, and some people thought Democrats in Illinois had broken the law to help Kennedy win. He beat Nixon in the state by fewer than 9,000 votes. Republicans thought Democrats might have also acted illegally in several other states, but they could not prove it. Kennedy was declared the winner and served as president from 1961 until his assassination in 1963.

believed that the government should spend as little money as possible and keep taxes low. They thought people should solve their problems on their own, rather than asking the government for help. In 1960, Hillary worked with local Republicans who were trying to challenge the Chicago election results that gave the presidency to Democrat John F. Kennedy. She went to city neighborhoods to see whether voters lived where they said they did. Four years later, she actively worked for Republican candidate Barry Goldwater when he ran for U.S. president.

But Hillary also heard Democratic views on current issues. She later said that her mother "was probably the only Democrat in Park Ridge, and probably a liberal Democrat." Mrs. Rodham had developed a strong belief in helping the poor and others with problems. Democrats, in general, wanted the government to work to solve those problems. Republicans thought private charities should help people who could not solve their problems on their own.

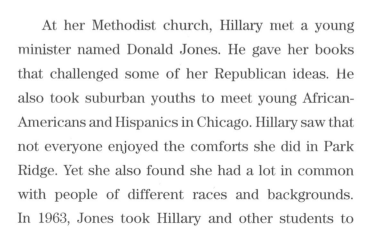

Hillary Rodham was photographed for her high school yearbook, Lens, *in 1965.*

At her Methodist church, Hillary met a young minister named Donald Jones. He gave her books that challenged some of her Republican ideas. He also took suburban youths to meet young African-Americans and Hispanics in Chicago. Hillary saw that not everyone enjoyed the comforts she did in Park Ridge. Yet she also found she had a lot in common with people of different races and backgrounds. In 1963, Jones took Hillary and other students to hear a speech by Martin Luther King Jr., a famous African-American minister and civil rights leader who was fighting for equal rights for blacks. Many conservatives opposed King's efforts. Though years later she remembered this speech as a highlight of her life, at the time Hillary remained a dedicated Republican with conservative views.

In June 1965, Hillary graduated from Maine Township High School South. Her classmates voted her "most likely to succeed." That fall, she entered Wellesley College, a women's college outside Boston, Massachusetts. At the time, some of the best U.S. universities, such as Harvard and Yale, did not accept female students. Wellesley was considered one of the best schools for young women. Hillary was excited to be starting college, but she felt lonely, overwhelmed, and out of place. Many of her classmates came from wealthy families and had gone to private schools.

At Wellesley, Hillary devoted herself to schoolwork and current affairs. She took courses in many subjects, but she enjoyed political science the most. A friend later remembered that instead of gossiping about boys, Hillary talked about the world's problems and how to solve them. For a time, she tutored a young African-American child from Boston. She also fought to change school rules that limited what Wellesley students could study and how much time they could spend with boys.

As a freshman, Hillary was chosen to lead the school's Young Republicans. In 1968, as a junior, she was elected president of the student government. That year, however, her political views took a drastic turn. Martin Luther King Jr. was assassinated. The country was also fighting a bloody war in Vietnam. Many college students opposed the war and protested the United States' role in it. Hillary began to support the Democratic Party and its strongest anti-war candidate, Senator Eugene McCarthy of Minnesota.

That summer, Hillary worked as an intern in Washington, D.C. Despite her new political views, she worked for Republicans in the U.S. House of Representatives. Before returning to school, Hillary and a friend went to Chicago, where Democrats chose Vice President Hubert Humphrey as their candidate

Hillary Rodham (center) was elected president of Wellesley student government.

In 1954, the Asian nation of Vietnam was split in two. North Vietnam had a communist government. The communist leaders of the Soviet Union supported North Vietnam's efforts to take over South Vietnam. The United States opposed the spread of communism and began sending military aid to South Vietnam. As many as 500,000 U.S. troops served in Southeast Asia at one time, and more than 58,000 were killed. Protests against the war influenced President Richard Nixon's decision to pull most U.S. troops out of Vietnam in 1973. Two years later, North Vietnam won the Vietnam War.

for U.S. president. Hillary watched in horror as police officers there battled young people who opposed the Vietnam War.

Hillary graduated in 1969 with a degree in political science. At her graduation ceremony, Hillary gave a speech to the students and their families. She was the first student ever to speak at a Wellesley graduation. Her speech reflected some of the new ideas she had developed in college. She defended young people who protested the war and other problems in the United States and ended her speech by saying, "the challenge now is to practice politics as the art of making what appears to be impossible, possible." She later recalled:

[The speech] reflected the countless conversations, questions, doubts and hopes each of us brought to that moment, not just as Wellesley graduates, but also as women and Americans whose lives would exemplify the changes and choices facing our generation at the end of the twentieth century.

Hillary Rodham received national attention for her graduation speech at Wellesley.

While a few members of the audience did not like her speech, most of her classmates clapped wildly when she finished. The Associated Press reported that she received a standing ovation lasting seven minutes. The speech drew national attention. Hillary's picture and part of her speech were printed in *Life*, a popular weekly magazine, and she appeared on a nationally broadcast television talk show.

Following a summer spent working at a salmon fishery in Alaska, Hillary prepared to enter Yale University Law School. She seemed headed for great things. ❧

Chapter

3 LEARNING THE LAW

࿇

Until 1968, few women were allowed to study at Yale University Law School. The college, located in New Haven, Connecticut, had accepted mostly white males for most of its history. When Hillary Rodham arrived there in the fall of 1969, she was one of 37 women in a class of 235 students.

As in high school and at Wellesley, Rodham worked hard in her courses. However, she also enjoyed spending time with her friends. Sometimes she made weekend trips to Vermont in an old car she nicknamed "Alphonse." There she visited David Rupert, one of her first serious boyfriends, whom she had met while working as an intern in Washington, D.C.

After her first year at Yale, Rodham returned

Hillary Rodham worked as an attorney with a House committee on President Nixon's impeachment case in 1974.

to Washington, D.C., to do research. She had met an African-American lawyer named Marian Wright Edelman, who worked on issues concerning the poor. For Edelman, Rodham began to do research on the education and health of migrant children, whose parents received low wages to work on U.S. farms. Her time with Edelman that summer and in the coming years changed Rodham's life. "The world opened up to me," she told a reporter in 1992, "and gave me a vision of what it ought to be." When she returned to Yale, Rodham decided to focus her studies on how the law affects children.

Marian Wright Edelman has worked for children's causes for nearly 40 years.

That second year at Yale, Rodham met another person who would influence the course of her life: Bill Clinton. Clinton was also a student at Yale. He knew Rodham was intelligent and one of the stars of her law school class. He followed her around for weeks but never approached her. Finally, she walked up to him in the library. "If you're going to keep looking at me," she said, "we might as well be introduced." As Rodham got to know Clinton, she saw his intelligence and ability to talk easily about many topics. Clinton had a knack for having fun and for making her laugh. With him, she was not as serious as she usually seemed to be. Like her, Clinton was devoted to politics and eager for a job that gave him power to change society for the better. He planned to return to his home state of Arkansas after law school to run for Congress.

In the summer of 1971, Rodham worked for a California law firm, and Clinton went west with her. When they returned to Connecticut in the fall, they rented an apartment together. Clinton was now a volunteer in the presidential campaign of Senator George McGovern. A Democrat from South Dakota, McGovern strongly opposed the Vietnam War. In the summer of 1972, Rodham also worked for McGovern. She joined Clinton in Texas, where she tried to persuade people between the ages of 18 and 21 to register to vote—and then to vote for McGovern.

For many years, the voting age in the United States was 21. During the Vietnam War, some Americans argued that if men under 21 could be required to fight in Vietnam, they should have a right to choose their political leaders. In 1971, the 26th Amendment to the U.S. Constitution, which lowered the voting age to 18, was ratified.

In May 1973, Rodham graduated from Yale University. That fall, she published her first article about the law in the *Harvard Educational Review*. In the article, "Children Under the Law," she argued that children should have the same legal rights in courts as adults. By this time, Rodham was working as a staff attorney for a legal organization called the Children's Defense Fund, which was run by her mentor, Marian Wright Edelman. She had moved to Cambridge, Massachusetts, while Clinton had returned to Arkansas to teach law. Rodham later wrote that during this time, "I missed Bill more than I could stand." She loved him, and he loved her, but Clinton's mother, Virginia Kelley, was not so sure about the match.

Virginia Kelley lived in Hot Springs, Arkansas. She loved to wear fancy clothes, put on makeup, tell jokes, and have a good time. For years, Clinton had introduced her to his girlfriends, most of whom were from the South. Kelley did not know what to think of Rodham. She wore plain clothes and no makeup, and she seemed serious all the time. She was also a "Yankee"—someone from the North. Clinton sensed that his mother did not like Rodham. But he told his mother, "I've had it up to here with beauty queens. I have to have somebody I can talk to."

By Christmas 1973, Rodham had decided to move to Arkansas, but a job opportunity kept her from going right away. John Doar, a lawyer Rodham had met at Yale, had just been hired by Congress. He wanted Rodham to help him with important legal work. Congress was considering whether to impeach President Richard Nixon. Nixon had known that some of his aides had orchestrated a break-in at an office used by Democrats. He had also secretly recorded all the conversations that took place in his

office, including conversations about the break-in
and what he knew about it. He refused to give the
tapes to government lawyers who were investigating
the break-in. The whole affair soon became known as
"Watergate," after the name of the building in which
the break-in took place.

*Hillary Rodham
helped John
Doar (stand-
ing, center)
and committee
members bring
impeachment
charges against
President
Richard Nixon
in 1974.*

Doar could not offer Rodham much money,
and she would have to work long hours. Still, she
could not turn down the chance. At 26, Rodham
was joining a team of lawyers that would help
Congress determine whether Nixon had engaged

in acts that were grounds for removal from office. As she later recalled, "I couldn't imagine a more important mission at this [point] in American history."

In Washington, D.C., Rodham sometimes worked 18 hours a day. She spent some of her time listening to the tapes Nixon had recorded. She also studied what might be considered an impeachable act. Rodham's work ended on August 9, 1974, when the president resigned rather than face impeachment.

During that summer, Rodham kept in touch with Clinton. He was running for a seat in the U.S. House of Representatives. Many who knew Rodham at this time remember her saying that her boyfriend would be president of the United States someday. She expected great things from Clinton and was willing to work hard to help him achieve them.

When her Watergate work ended, Rodham joined Clinton in Fayetteville, Arkansas. She started teaching law at the University of Arkansas and helped

The U.S. Constitution describes the process used to impeach a president. The U.S. House of Representatives must decide whether there is evidence that the president has broken the law. If there is, the Senate then acts as a jury, deciding whether the president is guilty or innocent. Before Watergate, Andrew Johnson was the only U.S. president to face an impeachment trial. He was found not guilty by just one vote. Nixon avoided impeachment by resigning as president. The only other president to face an impeachment trial was Bill Clinton, in 1999. He was found not guilty.

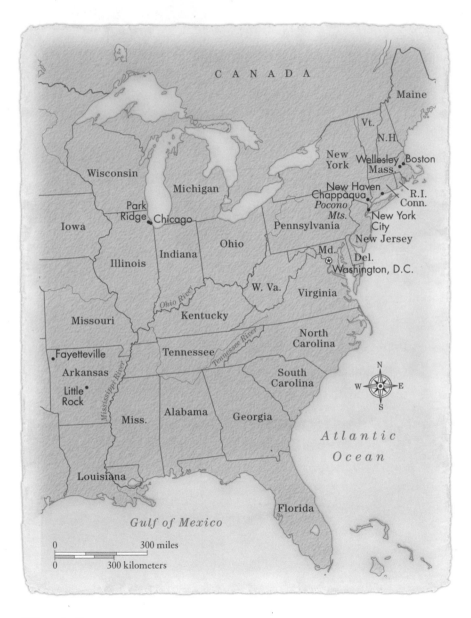

Hillary Rodham Clinton has lived in the Midwest and South, and on the East Coast.

run a legal-aid clinic. The clinic helped poor people who could not afford to hire lawyers. Rodham also helped Clinton with his campaign for Congress. She was determined that Clinton would win the race. In the end, however, he lost by 6,000 votes.

During the summer of 1975, Rodham spent time visiting friends in Chicago and on the East Coast. She was not sure what to do next with her life, and she considered working for major law firms in New York and Washington, D.C. When she returned to Fayetteville, Clinton had a surprise for her. He had bought a small house that she had once said she liked. Clinton wanted the two of them to live there— as husband and wife. Clinton had asked her to marry him before, and she had turned him down. This time, however, she said yes. She later admitted she was torn over what to do. Although she wanted to pursue her own career, she loved Clinton and knew she could help him with his goals. She told a reporter that in the end, "Bill's desire to be in public life was much more specific than my desire to do good." And she said, "I also knew that I had to deal with a whole other side of life, the emotional side, where we live and where we grow, and when all is said and done where the most important parts of life take place."

Bill Clinton and Hillary Rodham were married on October 11, 1975, in the living room of the house that Clinton had bought for them. As usual, Rodham had not thought about what she was going to wear. The day before the wedding, her mother took her to a local store, where Rodham grabbed the first dress she saw. Rodham stayed true to her feminist values by continuing to use her own last name, not Clinton's, after they were married. This decision upset her mother-in-law and others in Arkansas who believed in the tradition of a wife's taking her husband's last name.

The next year, Bill Clinton was elected attorney general of Arkansas. In that position, he represented the state in legal cases. Early in 1977, the couple moved to Little Rock, the state capital, so that Clinton could fulfill his duties as the state's attorney. Since his new job did not pay well, Rodham decided to leave teaching and work for a private company. Friends commented that Rodham had inherited her father's interest in saving and making sure the family had enough money for the future.

Rodham took a job with the Rose Law Firm, a major law office in Arkansas. One of the lawyers there was Vince Foster, who had known Bill Clinton since boyhood. Foster and Rodham became close friends. For the next two years, Rodham did legal research and argued a few cases in front of juries. But though she continued to build a successful career, her desire to do good never weakened. In late 1977, President Jimmy Carter appointed her to chair the board of directors of the Legal Services Corporation, a federal program that provided legal assistance to people who could not afford it. She also set up the Arkansas

Bill Clinton and Hillary Rodham, attending church in 1978, shared a strong Christian faith.

Advocates for Children and Families, an organization that tried to improve conditions for poor children in the state.

In 1978, Clinton ran for governor of Arkansas. Rodham once again helped him plan his campaign. Clinton impressed voters with his ideas, energy, and charm. He easily won the fall election. Hillary Rodham was Arkansas' new first lady. ❧

Chapter

4 FIRST LADY OF ARKANSAS

As the governor's wife, Hillary Rodham had many duties. Some of them were social, such as hosting events at the governor's mansion. Others were political. Clinton made her the head of a committee that studied health care issues in rural areas of Arkansas. She also took a strong interest in education—one of her husband's most important interests. Arkansas was a poor state, and its schools often lacked money. To raise funds, Governor Clinton hiked the fees people paid to register their cars.

Despite her new role, Rodham continued her law career. She told one Arkansas paper, "I need my own identity, too." In 1979, she became a partner, or part owner, in the Rose Law Firm. She also continued to do work for the Children's Defense Fund, as well as

Hillary Rodham spoke to reporters about the failure of her husband's 1980 campaign for a second term as governor.

the Legal Services Corporation.

That year, the Clintons decided to start a family. On February 27, 1980, Rodham gave birth to a daughter, Chelsea Victoria. She and Clinton named her after "Chelsea Morning," a song by Joni Mitchell that they both enjoyed. Rodham took four months off from work to be with Chelsea. She found motherhood to be both rewarding and challenging. As many babies do, Chelsea sometimes cried for long periods, despite her mother's efforts to stop her. Rodham would tell her daughter, "This is new for both of us. ... We're just going to have to help each other do the best we can." But the staff at the governor's mansion served as a built-in support network for Rodham, and the cook and other household workers soon came to be like family to Chelsea.

When Rodham returned to work, she began by working part time. She realized that most new parents were not fortunate enough to be able to do that and recognized the need for employers to give parents flexible work schedules and leave from work when a baby is born or adopted. This became an important issue for her. Years later, when her husband became president, the Family and Medical Leave Act was the first bill he signed.

Shortly after their daughter's birth, Rodham and Clinton were once again in the middle of a political campaign. The governor held office for two years at a

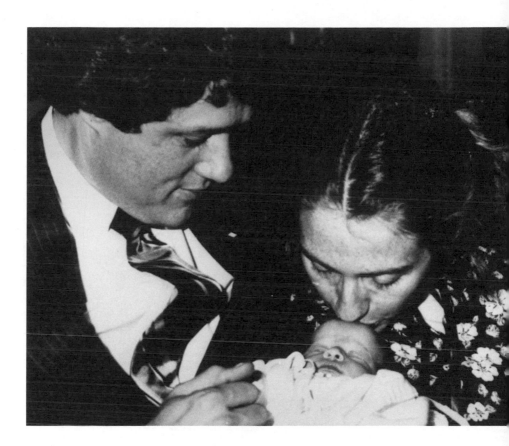

time, and Clinton wanted a second term. However, he had upset many Arkansas voters. The increased car registration fees upset some, and others thought he had failed to do everything he had promised during his first campaign. Rodham learned that she was also one of her husband's problems. Some voters could not accept a first lady who did not use her husband's last name and who had her own career.

In the fall of 1980, Clinton lost his re-election campaign for governor. He and his wife were stunned

The Clintons posed for a photo with their week-old daughter, Chelsea Victoria.

41

and saddened by the loss. For the next two years, Clinton worked at a Little Rock law firm, while Rodham continued to work at Rose. But they both knew Clinton would run for office again.

In 1982, Clinton again campaigned for governor. Rodham worked full time for her husband's cause. The Clinton family drove from one end of Arkansas to the other to meet voters. Rodham walked down streets and met voters with Chelsea on her hip or holding her hand. Rodham also decided to take her husband's last name, though she would still use her own as well. She would now be known as Hillary Rodham Clinton.

The whole family campaigned during Bill Clinton's governor's race.

As before, Hillary Rodham Clinton was an important part of her husband's campaign. She often served as his "attack dog," lashing out at his political opponents so he would not have to. When the sitting governor, Frank White, made campaign speeches, she often showed up to challenge his views. White said, "She'd put on the trial lawyer face and chop me up."

Bill Clinton easily defeated White, and as he prepared to take office, he told the public that this time he would govern differently. He had learned not to make a lot of promises he could not keep. But one promise he made again was to improve education in Arkansas. He asked his wife to lead that effort and appointed her to chair his new Educational Standards Committee.

Hillary Rodham Clinton traveled to every county in the state to talk to parents and teachers. She heard that some teachers themselves lacked basic skills, such as how to spell. She suggested that teachers be tested to make sure they were qualified. Students would also be tested before they moved from one grade to the next. She outlined her plan to Arkansas lawmakers. Afterward, one of them joked that voters might have elected the wrong Clinton.

Bill Clinton easily won his third term as governor in 1984, and he was re-elected to a fourth in 1986. This time, however, he would serve four years.

Hillary and Chelsea in 1984 Arkansas had just lengthened the governor's term of office. Hillary Rodham Clinton continued her work at the law firm, where she specialized in intellectual property, an area of the law that deals with protecting ideas and inventions. She also continued to do legal work for the welfare of children and was twice named by the *National Law Journal* as one of the 100 most influential lawyers in America. She also worked for several educational and legal organizations and joined the board of directors of Wal-Mart, the retail-store chain based in Arkansas. As a board member,

Clinton would help set the company's policies. She emphasized her reputation for trying to improve the status of women generally and promised that she would continue that work with the board. She also successfully pushed for the company to adopt more environmentally friendly practices.

By 1987, both Clinton and her husband had begun to think ahead. Ronald Reagan was almost at the end of his second term as president of the United States. By law, he could not run again in 1988. The Clintons briefly considered having Hillary run for Bill's job, but they decided against it. They also thought the time might be right for Bill to run for president.

The Clintons carefully weighed the benefits and drawbacks of a presidential campaign, and in July, Bill Clinton announced his decision. He surprised many by saying that he was not going to run for president. He later explained that he did not want to spend so much time away from Chelsea while she was still so young.

In 1988, the Democrats chose Governor Michael Dukakis of Massachusetts as their candidate. Bill Clinton gave a speech at the convention where Democrats officially gave Dukakis the nomination. For most Americans, this was their first chance to hear or see the Arkansas governor. His speech lasted a long time—too long, to most people. Some of the delegates began yelling at him to finish his speech.

He had flopped. Many political experts thought Bill Clinton's political career was over. But he won two more terms as governor, and in 1991, his wife told him he should again think about running for president. George H.W. Bush had beaten Dukakis in 1988 and was running for a second term. Hillary Rodham Clinton thought Bush was out of touch with many of the problems facing the country. She believed her husband could beat him, and so did some Democratic leaders.

In September 1991, Bill Clinton announced he was a candidate for his party's presidential nomination. Hillary Rodham Clinton later wrote:

Hillary Rodham Clinton helped her husband write many of his speeches. She suggested what ideas he should talk about and how to express them. One of the most important speeches she worked on was one Bill Clinton gave to the Democratic Leadership Council. This speech, which he made in 1991, convinced many Democrats that he had the talent to lead the nation.

We figured: What did we have to lose? Even if Bill's run failed, he would have the satisfaction of knowing he had tried, not just to win, but to make a difference for America. That seemed to be a risk worth taking.

But neither she nor her husband knew the difficulties that awaited them on the way to the White House.

5 IN THE PUBLIC EYE

಄ೕೕ಄

Soon after Bill Clinton decided to run for president, Hillary Rodham Clinton took a leave of absence from her law firm and began to hire people to help her during the campaign. She planned to make speeches and talk to reporters on her own to help her husband win votes. This was unusual behavior for a candidate's wife, but as she later wrote, she "was different—something that would become increasingly apparent in the months ahead."

Not many Americans knew much about the Clintons. They would have to explain who they were and what Bill Clinton hoped to do if he won the presidency. And they would need to be prepared for reporters digging into their past, looking for clues about their lives.

Hillary Rodham Clinton looked on as her husband was sworn in as president of the United States on January 20, 1993.

From the beginning, the process was difficult for the Clintons. For some time, the couple had faced rumors that Bill Clinton sometimes had relationships with women other than his wife. Clinton likely knew about these relationships, but she chose to ignore them. For Chelsea's sake and her husband's career, she wanted to keep the family together. However, with her husband now a presidential candidate, the rumors could no longer be ignored.

In January 1992 the Clintons appeared on the popular TV news show *60 Minutes* to discuss their lives together. They said that they had gone through difficult times, but they wanted to be married to each other. Most Americans seemed to agree that the Clintons' marriage was not the public's concern.

But other problems from the past continued to haunt the Clintons. In February, reporters began looking at Whitewater, a land-development deal the Clintons had been involved in. Bill Clinton had been governor of Arkansas at the time, and some people thought he had given his business partner special favors. The Clintons, however, said they had lost money on the Whitewater deal and that their partner had not gotten any favors from the state.

Clinton also denied charges that her law firm had been given state business because she was the governor's wife. She already had a successful and independent career, and she spoke out in defense

The Clintons had hoped to build a home on land in the Whitewater Estates.

of herself and other professional women who "tried to have an independent life and make a difference." She added, "You know, I suppose I could have stayed home and baked cookies and had teas, but what I decided to do was fulfill my profession, which I entered before my husband was in public life."

That comment angered many people with traditional ideas about families. They claimed that she was attacking women who chose to stay home and raise children. Clinton had often said that being a mother was the most important job she had ever had. She had been named Arkansas Mother of the Year in 1984. Now, however, many people turned against her as someone who held ideas most Americans did not accept.

As the campaign went on, the news media focused more attention on Clinton and highlighted

Long before the baby boomers appeared, feminists had argued that women deserved the same rights as men. In colonial times, most women could not sign contracts or own property, and women were not allowed to vote in all states until 1920. Many who opposed equality for women based their beliefs on the Bible. God, they said, created different roles for men and women. People who held these traditional views thought some feminists were a threat to families and their religious beliefs.

many of the issues women at the time faced. How did a mother juggle both a career and a family? What role should women play in business and politics? She later wrote, "I had been turned into a symbol for women of my generation. ... [E]verything I said or did—and even what I wore—became a hot button for debate."

Some people were also upset by a remark her husband had made. Bill Clinton claimed that, by electing him, voters could "buy one, get one free." Some people thought that Hillary Rodham Clinton would play too large a role in her husband's administration if he were elected. After one successful day during the Democratic primaries, she, not her husband, spoke first on a national news show.

The campaign led Clinton to assert herself as a mother. She wanted a "zone of privacy" around Chelsea. She did not want her daughter to be in media reports about her husband's campaign. Reporters could mention when Chelsea traveled with her parents and could take her picture with them. But

Chelsea would not take part in any interviews the Clintons gave.

In July, Bill Clinton won the Democratic nomination for president. He chose Senator Al Gore of Tennessee as his vice presidential running mate. Hillary Rodham Clinton joined the two men and Gore's wife, Tipper, on a bus trip across the country. They listened to the concerns of voters and explained why voters should choose Bill Clinton and Al Gore in November. At times, thousands of people came out to hear him speak and cheer him on. Hillary Rodham Clinton later wrote that the crowds created a joyous energy that she had never seen anywhere else in politics.

In November 1992, American voters elected Bill Clinton as the 42nd president of the United States,

Bill Clinton thanked his supporters after his presidential election victory in 1992.

defeating President George H.W. Bush and a Texas billionaire named Ross Perot. The Clintons were at home in Little Rock, surrounded by friends and family, when they learned their campaign had been successful. In his acceptance speech, Bill Clinton introduced his wife, saying that she would be one of the greatest first ladies in the history of the republic.

In preparation for her new role, Hillary Rodham Clinton studied the lives of past first ladies. She already knew about the important role Eleanor Roosevelt had played for her husband, Franklin. She learned about other first ladies who had been active in public affairs while their husbands held office. Abigail Adams, the wife of John Adams, had advised her husband on political issues. President Woodrow Wilson's wife Edith had practically run the government in 1919, when the president was sick. And Bess Truman, wife of Harry S. Truman, reviewed her husband's speeches and letters.

The Clintons had almost three months to prepare for their new lives as president and first lady. Hillary Rodham Clinton arranged to move all the family's belongings from Arkansas to the White House, and she found a school for 12-year-old Chelsea. She also thought about her duties as first lady. She knew she would play an active role in the Clinton administration.

On January 20, 1993, Bill Clinton was sworn in as president of the United States. The day was a festive one, as Democrats celebrated the country's new leader. That evening, the Clintons arrived at the White House. Hillary Rodham Clinton had often seen the White House, and

The Clintons attended all 11 inaugural balls held in their honor.

she had been inside as a guest of several presidents. Now, this landmark of United States history was going to be her home. The reality of the situation finally hit her. She later said, "I was actually the First Lady, married to the President of the United States. It was the first of many times I would be reminded of the history I was now joining." ♌

6 In the White House

Soon after the Clintons came to Washington, D.C., a joke about them went around the Internet: Driving together in Hillary Rodham Clinton's hometown, they meet a man she once dated. He is working in a gas station. Her husband teases her, asking her to imagine what her life would be like if she had married the old boyfriend instead of him. She replies, "If I'd married him, you'd be pumping gas, and he'd be president."

The joke reflected the belief that Bill Clinton could not have become president without his wife's political abilities. Some people, however, still were not sure they wanted her playing an active role in the government. The Clintons knew this, but they also knew the first lady's talents should not be wasted. President Clinton decided to put his wife in charge

First lady Hillary Rodham Clinton spoke with reporters after testifying before a grand jury investigating Whitewater.

> *Early in 1993, Hillary Rodham Clinton met with Jacqueline Kennedy Onassis, who had been married to President John F. Kennedy and was perhaps the most popular first lady ever. Clinton asked for her advice on preserving the privacy of herself and her daughter. Clinton also had imaginary talks with Eleanor Roosevelt. She had always respected Mrs. Roosevelt and thought these "chats" would help her get through difficult times.*

of a task force to study health care in the United States. With her new job, Hillary Rodham Clinton became the first president's wife to take a government position.

In 1993, by most estimates, about 40 million Americans lacked health insurance. The Clintons wanted to create a system that provided health care to all Americans. Hillary Rodham Clinton hoped to find a way to improve health care and win the support of political and business leaders.

By the end of that year, she had put together a complex proposal that required employers to provide health care for all employees through health maintenance organizations, or HMOs. The bill was presented to Congress in November 1993. It faced heavy opposition. Many thought it was unrealistic and overreaching. New York Senator Daniel Patrick Moynihan said, "Anyone who thinks [the Clinton plan] can work in the real world as presently written isn't living in it." A 1994 compromise bill couldn't keep the plan afloat, and her plan for health care reform died soon after. The plan, which opponents referred to

as "Hillarycare," became for many an example of big government.

Clinton was working on her health care plan in the midst of several White House controversies. After learning of mistakes made by the White House travel office, she urged an aide to dismantle the travel office and offer the work to friends from Arkansas instead.

Clinton (right) was part of a panel discussion on health care in the United States.

After the Watergate scandal, which Clinton had helped investigate after law school, the media often added "gate" to any presidential scandal. This incident soon became known as "Travelgate." People believed that Clinton had unfairly used her power as first lady to attack the White House travel office and help her friends.

Hillary Rodham Clinton's troubles continued throughout her first year in Washington, D.C. By the end of the year, the media were again looking at the Clintons' old Whitewater business dealings. President Clinton was under pressure to start an investigation to make sure he and his wife had not broken any laws. In January 1994, he agreed to the investigation, which was led by attorney Kenneth Starr.

Clinton believed that conservatives who opposed her husband's administration were the cause of many of their problems. "It didn't matter that we had done nothing wrong," she later wrote. "It only mattered that the public was given the impression that we had." Whitewater in particular, she believed, was "a political war." The Whitewater investigation would continue for the next eight years. Although two of their business partners did end up in jail, Clinton was never charged with any crime, and no evidence was found that she or her husband had done anything wrong.

In her private life, Clinton also faced problems.

Her father, Hugh Rodham, died soon after the Clintons settled in Washington, D.C. In July, her aide and old friend Vince Foster killed himself. He had been battling depression for some time, and his new government duties overwhelmed him. So did the media attention the administration received.

Kenneth Starr spoke to reporters during his investigation of the Clintons' involvement in the Whitewater land-development deal.

Despite their problems, the Clintons continued to carry out their duties as president and first lady. While President Clinton worked on the economy and peace in the Middle East, the first lady worked on health care issues. She also represented the United States at international events. In February 1994, she and Chelsea went to Norway for the Winter Olympic Games. In June, she and her husband traveled to England to honor the 50th anniversary of an important World War II battle. On these and other travels, she met world leaders and discussed foreign affairs.

One of the first lady's most important trips came in 1995, when she attended the United Nations Fourth World Conference on Women, held in Beijing, China. She gave a speech on women's rights, and although she had given thousands of speeches, she was nervous before this one. "I was speaking as a representative of my country," she later wrote. "The stakes were high."

In the speech she gave, Clinton emphasized the importance of women's rights as the foundation for a healthy society, saying:

The United Nations was founded in 1945. President Franklin Roosevelt worked hard to create this international group, which tries to prevent wars and solve the world's problems. More than 190 nations belong to the organization, which has its headquarters in New York City.

If women have a chance to [be] full and equal partners in society, their families will flourish. And when families flourish, communities and nations will flourish. ... If there is one message that echoes forth from this conference, let it be that human rights are women's rights. And women's rights are human rights, once and for all.

After that speech, she received many invitations from around the world to speak on women's issues. The president later called the speech "one of the most important ... delivered by anyone in our administration."

Prominent women representing many nations attended the U.N. Conference on Women in Beijing, China.

Still, personal problems continued to plague the Clintons. The continuing attention to Whitewater and her role in it was creating pressure on the first lady. In January 1996, she received a subpoena requiring her to appear before a grand jury. The grand jury would decide whether there was enough evidence to suspect that the Clintons had broken any laws. The first lady told reporters that she would do anything to cooperate and to bring the matter to a close. And on January 26, 1996, she once again made history as the only first lady to appear in front of a grand jury.

In the months that followed, Clinton toured the country to campaign for her husband's re-election. As she traveled, she met many women who supported her and her work as first lady. They admired her for her intelligence, hard work, and success as both a career woman and mother. During 1996, the first lady helped raise more than $11 million for her husband's campaign. Most of it came from women.

This time, President Clinton's opponent for president was Republican Senator Bob Dole. Once again, Ross Perot ran as well. President Clinton told voters he would protect education, the environment, and government programs that offered health care to the poor and elderly. Dole and the Republicans, he warned, would damage those programs. In November, the voters chose

In 1996, Clinton published a book called It Takes a Village and Other Lessons Children Teach Us. *In the book, she discusses her childhood, her experiences with her daughter, Chelsea, and what Americans should do to improve the lives of their children. The title comes from an African proverb, "It takes a village to raise a child." The audio recording she made of the book won a Grammy Award for Best Spoken Word Album in 1997.*

Ten-year-old Daniela Fortuna introduced Clinton during a 1996 tour to promote her book, It Takes a Village and Other Lessons Children Teach Us.

Bill Clinton as president for the second time. Hillary Rodham Clinton would have four more years as the first lady of the United States. ❧

Chapter

7 PERSONAL AND POLITICAL CRISIS

❦

In the weeks before her husband's second inauguration, Hillary Rodham Clinton thought about what she wanted to do during his second term. Working on problems that affected women and children was at the top of her list. During the first term, she had studied the difficulties many working mothers faced. They often could not afford day care for their children. Many children also lacked the chance to begin learning before entering school. Clinton knew that children should be read to at an early age, but many parents did not have the time to do this with their children. The first lady hoped to use her influence in Congress and with the president to make sure programs for women and children received money.

Hillary Rodham Clinton's official portrait as first lady is on display in the White House.

> *Nelson Mandela (1918–) was imprisoned for 27 years for leading a rebel army trying to end a system called apartheid. A small number of white South Africans had controlled the country for centuries. Blacks could only hold low-paying jobs and could not vote. In the 1980s, some countries began to protest apartheid. Mandela was released in 1990, and apartheid ended the next year. In 1994, he was chosen the country's first black president.*

Early in 1997, Clinton and her daughter took a trip to Africa. She gave several speeches on women's rights. She visited tourist attractions, such as Victoria Falls, one of the largest waterfalls in the world. Clinton and her daughter also met with Nelson Mandela, the president of South Africa. The first lady admired his long struggle to end apartheid, a system of racist practices.

Back at home, Clinton fulfilled the traditional duties of the first lady. She welcomed visiting leaders and their wives and hosted state dinners. She restored or redecorated several rooms in the White House. She also started a program called Save America's Treasures, which raised money to preserve and restore historic sites and artifacts, including the flag that inspired the song "The Star-Spangled Banner." And she continued to speak out on women's rights and other topics.

She also tried to find time to be alone with her husband and daughter. In August 1997, they vacationed on Martha's Vineyard, a small island off

Clinton and her daughter, Chelsea, met with Nelson Mandela at his home in Cape Town during their 1997 tour of South Africa.

the coast of Massachusetts. The family had first visited there in 1993 and found it a quiet place to relax with friends. When summer ended, the Clintons took Chelsea to California, where she was starting her first year at Stanford University. The first lady did not like her daughter's going so far from home for college. But the president reminded her that they had agreed Chelsea should go where she wanted. And, of course, she would be protected by the Secret Service agents who always followed her and her parents.

Through all this, the Whitewater investigations continued to drag on. Kenneth Starr also began

69

The Clintons joined their daughter at an orientation event at Stanford University.

looking into other issues involving the Clintons. News reports claimed that President Clinton had lied to attorneys about his relationship with a White House intern named Monica Lewinsky. The president denied there had been an affair, and Lewinsky did as well.

Starr believed that President Clinton and Lewinsky had lied under oath, which is a crime called perjury. The president warned his wife that the newspapers would have the story about Lewinsky, but he told her that the news was not true.

The first lady wrestled with her emotions. Before this, she had thought her husband's political problems were coming to an end. Now he faced impeachment if Starr proved that he had lied under oath.

The first lady appeared on TV to defend her husband. She also kept up her busy schedule of speeches and meetings. Through the first nine months of the year, she went back to Africa and China. She also spoke at colleges and historic sites across the United States. But Starr's ongoing investigations were always on her mind.

In August, Bill Clinton finally admitted what he had dreaded saying. He told his wife that he had lied before. He had been involved with Lewinsky. The first lady was heartbroken and angry—more upset than she had ever been before. She spoke with Don Jones, the Methodist minister she had known in high school. He offered her advice, and she took comfort in her religious beliefs. Clinton decided she would stay with her husband and defend him. The couple started going to a counselor to discuss the problems in their marriage. And President Clinton planned to tell the country he had lied about Lewinsky. He hoped the American people would forgive him, but both Clintons knew that some people would demand the impeachment of the president.

In late September 1998, Hillary Rodham Clinton met with Democratic lawmakers to plan how to fight impeachment. She drew on her experience working on the Watergate impeachment hearings almost

Monica Lewinsky (center left) was led through news photographers to her lawyer's office in July 1998.

25 years earlier. She did not believe that anything her husband had done amounted to "high crimes and misdemeanors," the words used in the U.S. Constitution to define the kind of acts that call for impeachment. One lawmaker admired her fighting spirit. He told a reporter, "If I was going to war, I'd want her covering my rear. She's never going to run from a fight."

In October, the House of Representatives voted to investigate President Clinton's activities. By this time, the first lady was traveling often. Congressional elections were approaching, and she wanted to make sure voters elected Democrats. Clinton flew so often during this period that she developed a blood clot in one of her legs. Such clots can develop during long air flights and can be deadly if they move into the heart. A nurse began traveling with her, to make sure she took the medicine she needed to get rid of the clot. She refused, however, to stop her travels. Once again, the first lady's efforts helped the Democrats raise millions of dollars and elect more lawmakers than some people had expected.

In Congress, however, the impeachment investigation continued. Eventually the House charged the president with lying under oath and trying to keep Kenneth Starr from learning the truth.

In January 1999, the Senate met to consider the charges. Unlike many Americans, the first lady did not watch the trial on TV. She knew she could not do anything to change the result. Still, she had faith that her husband would not be convicted. Under the Constitution, 67 of the 100 members had to find Clinton guilty for him to be convicted and removed from office. On the charge of perjury, 45 senators said the president was guilty. On the second charge, 50 said he was guilty. The president had survived.

When he learned the news, President Clinton once again told the nation he was sorry about what had happened. But his wife was not with him. In another part of the White House, Hillary Rodham Clinton was beginning to think about her own political career. ℘

8 NEW YORK CALLS

❦

As early as 1997, people had approached Hillary Rodham Clinton about running for the U.S. Senate. New York seemed like a possible site for her first political campaign. Although she had never lived there, the first lady was popular in the state. Judith Hope, a Democratic leader in New York, had suggested that Clinton run there. The first lady dismissed the idea.

In November 1998, Democrat Daniel Patrick Moynihan, one of New York's two senators, announced that he would not seek re-election in 2000. More Democrats in the state began to suggest that Clinton would make an excellent candidate. A January 1999 article in *The Washington Post* discussed her popularity in the state. Though an aide denied rumors, some reporters and political experts

First lady Hillary Rodham Clinton waded through a sea of children at a middle school during a stop on her "listening tour" of New York.

Clinton joked with Daniel Patrick Moynihan, the senator whose seat she hoped to win.

thought the first lady had already decided that she would run. And the president himself said that he thought his wife would make a terrific senator.

The news media began to report on Clinton's actions as if she had already decided to run for the Senate. Things she said and did in public were examined to see how they might affect voters in New York. In actuality, the first lady was still very much focused on her husband's impeachment trial. But on the day the Senate found President Clinton not guilty, she met with Harold Ickes, an expert on politics in New York. They talked for hours about what a campaign would be like and what she would have to do to win.

Friends warned her that a campaign would be difficult and unpleasant. The media would focus on her past problems and attack her as a "carpetbagger." This term was first used after the Civil War to describe Northerners who went into the South to become active in politics. Today it means someone who moves to a state where he or she sees a good opportunity for election. Clinton would also face a tough opponent—popular New York City mayor Rudolph Giuliani.

Clinton did not announce that she was planning to run. But by February 1999, she began to make frequent trips to New York and started to raise money for a possible campaign. In her mind, the good things she could do as a U.S. senator seemed more important than the difficulties of a campaign. She thought about all the times she had told other women to take action, especially in politics. She later wrote, "How could I pass up an opportunity to do the same?"

New York's most famous "carpetbagger" before Hillary Rodham Clinton was Robert F. Kennedy. The brother of President John F. Kennedy, he ran for the Senate in New York in 1964. A native of Massachusetts, he won the race in New York and then ran for the Democratic presidential nomination in 1968. He was shot and killed during the campaign.

In July, Clinton formed a committee to explore whether she should run for the Senate in New York. She also began what she called a "listening tour," which would help her learn what issues were important to voters and what they expected from her if she won the race. She soon learned that some New Yorkers did not like the idea of an outsider representing their state. When the first lady appeared, protesters met her with signs that

Clinton campaigned at a union picnic in Pomona, New York.

said such things as "Hillary Listen: Go Home!" She appeared on national television several times, making jokes and trying to improve her image. Friends had often said that in private she was fun-loving and liked to laugh. Most Americans, however, had never seen that side of the first lady. They seemed to think she was pushy and cold.

Before she could begin an official campaign for New York's Senate seat, Clinton had to first become a resident of New York. In September 1999, she and her husband bought a home in Chappaqua, a small town about 25 miles (40 kilometers) north of New York City. Since they had lived in the governor's mansion in Arkansas and then the White House, this was the first home the Clintons had owned in 20 years. The following February, as a new resident of New York state, Hillary Rodham Clinton officially announced her decision to run for the Senate. She admitted that she was "new to the neighborhood," but she told voters, "I'm not new to your concerns." She said she would focus on education, health care, and economic issues.

The first lady faced a tough opponent. Rudy Giuliani had won praise for his work as mayor of New York City. He had also raised a lot of money for his Senate campaign. But in May, Giuliani pulled out of the race after learning he had cancer. To replace him, New York Republicans chose U.S. Representative Rick Lazio.

That fall, Lazio and Clinton held three debates. Entering the first debate, they were virtually tied in opinion polls. Lazio was clearly more conservative than the first lady. He called for cutting taxes and ending government rules that limited the freedom of some businesses. He said Clinton was too liberal, and along with other Republicans, kept repeating the carpetbagger charge.

New York Mayor Rudy Giuliani (left) pulled out of the Senate race and was replaced by U.S. Representative Rich Lazio (right).

In the end, Clinton won the race—and made history. She became the first woman to win a statewide election in New York and the only first lady to win a national political office. After her win, Clinton promised New Yorkers, "I will do everything I can to be worthy of your faith and trust."

The 2000 election was not completely satisfying to Clinton, though. Her husband had served his two terms as president, and so Vice President Al Gore ran as the Democratic Party's presidential candidate. Gore won the popular vote but lost to Republican George W. Bush, son of former President George H.W. Bush, in the Electoral College. The election was extremely close, and the U.S. Supreme Court had to step in to end a legal battle questioning the results in Florida.

The next few months were hectic for the Clintons. They had to move out of the White House and into their home in Chappaqua. Clinton also had to hire the aides she would need as a senator. On January 3, 2001, she officially began her new job. A little more than two weeks later, she left the White House for the last time as first lady. She later wrote, "I said goodbye to the house where I had spent eight years living history." Now she would begin making history in the U.S. Senate. ☙

9 NEW CHALLENGES

As a U.S. senator, Hillary Rodham Clinton divided her time between Washington, D.C., and New York. In her new home state, she continued to meet with voters and hear their concerns. In the Senate, she was appointed to several important committees, including one dealing with health, education, labor, and public works. Later, she was named to the Armed Services Committee, which deals with the military.

During her first year in the Senate, she and the nation experienced a horrible event. On September 11, 2001, members of a terrorist group called al-Qaeda flew two planes into New York City's World Trade Center. Another plane crashed into the Pentagon, the U.S. military headquarters, just outside of Washington, D.C. A fourth plane crashed in a field

Senator Clinton hopes to become the first female president of the United States.

in Pennsylvania. Nearly 3,000 people were killed in the attacks.

Clinton was familiar with al-Qaeda. Its members had committed terrorist acts during her husband's presidency. The attacks on September 11, however, were the worst ever against the United States. The next day, she spoke about the killings. "This was an attack on New York," she said, "but it was really an attack on America." She traveled to New York City to see the damage and help the city prepare to rebuild.

Terrorists flew commercial airplanes into both towers of New York City's World Trade Center on September 11, 2001.

In the months that followed, Clinton supported President Bush's efforts to fight the terrorists. She approved sending U.S. troops to Afghanistan, where al-Qaeda trained its terrorists, and called for tightening U.S. borders so terrorists could not easily enter the country. And knowing that New York City could be the target of future attacks, she wanted more money spent there on anti-terrorist efforts. In 2002, President Bush declared that Iraq was helping terrorists, and in March 2003, the president sent troops into Iraq. Once again, Clinton supported the president.

Terrorism and war were not the only issues Senator Clinton faced. She worked for laws that gave New York money for such things as transportation and health care. She also proposed laws dealing with cleaning the environment and providing medical care to members of the National Guard.

During her first two years in the

On March 20, 2003, U.S. airplanes began bombing Baghdad, the capital of Iraq. Soon after, U.S. troops entered the nation. Within six weeks, the United States and its allies controlled Iraq, and President George W. Bush declared major military actions over. But some Iraqis, joined by foreign terrorists, resisted the effort to set up a government friendly to the United States. By 2007, more than 3,000 Americans had been killed in the conflict. Americans also learned that Bush and his advisers had been wrong about the danger Iraq posed to the United States. That fact, the cost of the war, and the number of soldiers killed and wounded led many Americans to call for the removal of U.S. troops from Iraq.

Senate, Clinton did not speak out often. She tried to work behind the scenes and win the trust of the other members of the Senate, both Republicans and Democrats. One senator said, "She works extremely hard. … I've been around really strong, able people, and she's at the top."

In the summer of 2003, Senator Clinton toured the country to promote her autobiography, *Living History*. She gave many interviews and spoke at bookstores. Tens of thousands of people lined up to see her and buy copies of the book.

Clinton signed copies of her autobiography, Living History. *Her audio recording of the book was nominated for a Grammy Award for Best Spoken Word Album.*

By this time, Chelsea Clinton had graduated from Stanford, studied in England, and moved to New York City. She took a job dealing with international relations. Bill Clinton was often traveling, giving speeches around the world. With her husband and daughter busy with their own lives, Clinton could focus all her energy on her own duties as a senator. On a typical day in Washington, D.C., she might meet with people representing various groups of New Yorkers, ranging from farmers to business owners to retired people. She might then fly to New York for meetings with local officials. Lunch could include a speech to a business or political group. Her work usually continued into the evening, when she might make another speech or attend a public event. And throughout the day, the senator would be on the phone with her aides. Clinton loved the hard work of being a senator. She told one reporter, "I'm having the time of my life."

As the 2004 elections approached, some political experts wondered if Clinton would run for president. The senator said she was happy in the

In addition to Living History and 1996's It Takes a Village and Other Lessons Children Teach Us, Clinton has written two other books. One features letters written to the Clintons' "first pets," Socks the Cat and Buddy the Dog. The other, An Invitation to the White House, shows the inner workings of the White House and describes some of the people who visited the Clintons there.

Senate. She and her husband backed Senator John Kerry when the Democrats chose him as their candidate. Just as she had done for her husband, Clinton helped raise money for Kerry's campaign. Many of her fundraising events took place in Washington, D.C., at the second home the Clintons had bought several years earlier. She also traveled the country, speaking for Kerry and other Democratic candidates. Her efforts, however, were not enough. Kerry could not defeat President Bush. The Republicans also kept control of Congress.

Senator Clinton and Teresa Heinz Kerry campaigned in support of the 2004 Democratic presidential nominee, Massachusetts Senator John Kerry.

Clinton and the Democrats would remain in the minority, but already some of them were thinking about future elections.

With Kerry's defeat, talk began that Clinton would run for president in 2008. Throughout the senator's adult life, many close to her had come to believe she had the skills to become the first female president of the United States. She was intelligent and hardworking, and she cared about people. She also understood politics and knew when to be tough.

As Clinton raised money for her 2006 re-election campaign, Democrats began to pledge to support her if she ran for president. And more Republicans had come to respect her, even if they did not agree with her on all the issues. These included members of the health care industry who had opposed her efforts to change health care policy in 1993. As a senator, Clinton impressed them with her knowledge of the health care system. She also showed a willingness to consider the interests of doctors and not seek drastic changes. Some of the Republicans working in health care who had once attacked her now gave money to help her win re-election in 2006.

Her Republican opponent in the Senate race was John Spencer, the former mayor of Yonkers, New York. The senator easily won the election, even winning in towns that usually voted for Republicans.

Back in the Senate, Clinton turned to the one issue most Americans worried about: the ongoing war in Iraq. She had always supported President Bush's requests for money to fund the war, but she began to think he did not have a good plan to end it. Even before the 2006 election, she questioned some of Bush's moves in foreign policy. She said, "We need to return to patient diplomacy." She, like other Americans, had begun to think Bush had rushed into the war with Iraq. But she still believed the country needed a strong military and should react quickly to terrorist threats.

Senator Clinton traveled to Iraq and was given a tour of the military living quarters.

As 2006 ended, more political experts expected Clinton to announce she was running for president in 2008. That word finally came on January 20, 2007—and in an unusual way. Instead of making a speech to a cheering crowd, Clinton sent an e-mail message to her supporters. She told them, "I'm in. And I'm in to win." She also posted a video on her Web site explaining her decision.

Clinton, however, was not the first Democrat to enter the race. Just the week before, Senator Barack Obama of Illinois had announced his candidacy. Obama had only been in the Senate two years, but he had already won many supporters. Unlike Clinton, he had opposed the Iraq war even before it was launched. For many Democrats, strongly opposing the war and seeking a quick end to it were key issues.

Clinton was speaking out more against the war as well. Just a week before she announced her candidacy, she said, "I don't know that the American people or the Congress at this point believe this mission can work." Yet Clinton did not believe she had made a mistake in 2002 when she voted to give President Bush the power to go to war with Iraq.

Clinton knew the whole world was watching her campaign. Her relationship with Bill Clinton and her own political career had always fascinated both her supporters and opponents. Through 2007, more

Clinton joked with Barack Obama, a fellow senator and candidate for the Democratic presidential nomination, at a presidential debate in 2007.

than 40 books had been written about her. Many were not favorable, and some were even hostile. Still, no one doubted that Clinton was ambitious, and many believed she could be a good president. And despite her fame and everything that was written about her, she remained at heart a private person. She often said she may be the most famous woman nobody really knows.

People closely watched her campaign precisely because she was a woman. No woman had ever come close to winning the presidency. The senator told one crowd of supporters, "I expect there will be more stories about my clothes and hair than the other people running." But polls showed that just over half of voters would consider voting for the former first lady if she won the Democratic nomination.

As her campaign went on, Clinton outlined what she hoped to do if she won the presidency. She was concerned with the growing gap in wealth between the richest and poorest Americans. She called for giving less government aid to large businesses and helping companies that created new jobs. Clinton also wanted affordable health care for everyone, and aid to students who wanted to go to college. As always, education was a key issue for her. She argued that a 21st century education starts early in life and continues well into adulthood. She also promised to bring U.S. troops home from Iraq within the first

Women first ran for U.S. president even before they had the right to vote. In 1872, the Equal Rights Party chose Victoria Woodhull as its candidate for president. The party nominated Belva Ann Lockwood in 1884 and 1888. In 1964, Republican Senator Margaret Chase Smith became the first woman to seek the nomination of a major political party. She was followed by three female Democrats in 1972. The most successful was Shirley Chisholm, an African-American member of Congress.

Senator Clinton gave the crowd a thumbs-up before a town hall meeting in Des Moines, Iowa.

100 days of her presidency.

Through 2007, Senator Clinton traveled across the United States. At times, she also debated the candidates who opposed her for the Democratic nomination. She spoke to cheering crowds and raised money for her campaign. She explained her vision for the country:

> *I am running for president because I believe if we set big goals and we work together to achieve them, we can restore the American dream today and for the next generation.*

Hillary Rodham Clinton has held many important roles in her life, and she has broken ground in most of them. No matter what happens in her future, first lady and Senator Hillary Rodham Clinton has already secured her spot as one of the most powerful women ever in U.S. politics. ❧

CLINTON'S LIFE

1965
Enters Wellesley
College

1969
Graduates from
college, becoming
the first student at
Wellesley to speak
at graduation; enters
Yale University Law
School in the fall

1947
Born October 26 in
Chicago, Illinois

1945

1945
The United Nations is
founded; 50 nations
sign the charter

1962
Pope John XXIII calls
the Second Vatican
Council, modernizing
Roman Catholicism

1969
U.S. astronauts are
the first humans to
land on the moon

WORLD EVENTS

1974

Works for the committee investigating whether President Richard Nixon should be impeached; moves to Arkansas and begins teaching law

1975

Marries Bill Clinton

1973

Graduates from Yale University Law School

1970

1974

Scientists find that chlorofluorocarbons—chemicals in coolants and propellants—are damaging Earth's ozone layer

1973

Spanish artist Pablo Picasso dies

1971

The first microprocessor is produced by Intel

CLINTON'S LIFE

1978

Becomes the first lady of Arkansas when her husband is elected governor

1977

Begins working for the Rose Law Firm

1980

Gives birth to daughter, Chelsea

1975

1978

The first test-tube baby conceived outside its mother's womb is born in Oldham, England

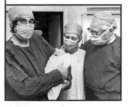

1976

U.S. military academies admit women

WORLD EVENTS

1983

Leads a government
program to improve
education in Arkansas

1993

Becomes first lady
of the United States
when her husband
is elected president;
works to solve the
country's health care
problems

1995

Gives an important
speech in China on
the rights of women

1990

1987

Stock markets fall sharply
around the world on Black
Monday, October 19

1994

Genocide of 500,000
to 1 million of the
minority Tutsi group
by rival Hutu people
in Rwanda

1983

The AIDS (acquired
immune deficiency
syndrome) virus
is identified

CLINTON'S LIFE

1998

Defends her
husband as he
faces impeachment

2000

Elected a U.S. sena-
tor from New York,
becoming the only
first lady ever to
hold a national
political office

2001

Supports a U.S. invasion
of Afghanistan following
the September 11 terrorist
attacks and calls for more
government spending to
prevent future attacks

2000

1996

A sheep is cloned
in Scotland

2001

September 11 terrorist
attacks on the two
World Trade Center
Towers in New York City
and on the Pentagon in
Washington, D.C., leave
thousands dead

WORLD EVENTS

2003

Travels the country to promote her autobiography, *Living History*

2006

Re-elected to a second term as a U.S. senator

2007

Announces her candidacy for the presidency in the 2008 election

2005

2003

The U.S. space shuttle *Columbia* explodes, killing all seven astronauts on board

2005

The Kyoto Protocol, an international treaty on climate change, goes into effect without the support of the United States and Australia

2007

Former Vice President Al Gore and a United Nations panel on climate change win the Nobel Peace Prize for their efforts to spread awareness of global warming

DATE OF BIRTH: October 26, 1947

BIRTHPLACE: Chicago, Illinois

FATHER: Hugh Rodham Jr.
(1911–1993)

MOTHER: Dorothy Howell Rodham
(1919–)

EDUCATION: Bachelor's degree from
Wellesley College and
law degree from Yale
University Law School

SPOUSE: William Jefferson Clinton
(1946–)

DATE OF MARRIAGE: October 11, 1975

CHILDREN: Chelsea Victoria (1980–)

IN THE LIBRARY

Anthony, Carl Sferrazza. *America's Most Influential First Ladies.* Minneapolis: Oliver Press, 2003.

Gullo, Jim. *Hillary Rodham Clinton.* San Diego: Lucent Books, 2004.

Landau, Elaine. *Friendly Foes: A Look at Political Parties.* Minneapolis: Lerner Publishing Company, 2004.

Wagner, Heather Lehr. *Hillary Rodham Clinton.* Philadelphia: Chelsea House, 2004.

LOOK FOR MORE SIGNATURE LIVES
BOOKS ABOUT THIS ERA:

Cesar Chavez: *Heroic Crusader for Social Change*

Elizabeth Dole: *Public Servant and Senator*

Thomas Alva Edison: *Great American Inventor*

Wilma Mankiller: *Chief of the Cherokee Nation*

Thurgood Marshall: *Civil Rights Lawyer and Supreme Court Justice*

Eleanor Roosevelt: *First Lady of the World*

Franklin Delano Roosevelt: *The New Deal President*

Elizabeth Cady Stanton: *Social Reformer*

Gloria Steinem: *Champion of Women's Rights*

Madam C.J. Walker: *Entrepreneur and Millionaire*

Booker T. Washington: *Innovative Educator*

ON THE WEB

For more information on this topic, use FactHound.

1. Go to *www.facthound.com*
2. Type in this book ID: 0756515882
3. Click on the *Fetch It* button.

FactHound will find the best
Web sites for you.

HISTORIC SITES

Clinton Presidential Library and Museum
1200 President Clinton Ave.
Little Rock, AR 72201
501/374-4242
Exhibit feature items from the Clinton
administration

The United States Capitol
Constitution Avenue and First Street N.W.
Washington, DC 20002
202/225-6827
Where the U.S. Senate and U.S. House
of Representatives meet to make and
pass laws

administration
the officials and actions connected to a particular U.S. president

conservatives
in politics, people who want to avoid major changes and keep business and industry in private hands

feminist
a person who supports equal rights for women in all parts of society

impeachment
a process for charging a government official with misconduct while in office

inauguration
the ceremony at which a president is sworn into office

intern
a person who works with little or no pay to gain experience at a particular job

liberal
a person who favors a political philosophy of progress and reform and protection of civil liberties

media
businesses that report the news

subpoena
a legal document that forces someone to appear before a judge or jury

Chapter 1

Page 9, line 10: "It's Official: Hillary Clinton Announces Senate Candidacy." CNN.com. 6 Feb. 2000. 26 Oct. 2007. http://archives.cnn.com/2000/ALLPOLITICS/stories/02/06/hillary.announce.01/index.html

Page 12, line 15: Hillary Rodham Clinton. *Living History.* New York: Simon and Schuster, 2003, p. 523.

Chapter 2

Page 17, lines 25 and 28: Ibid., p. 12.

Page 18, line 28: David Maraniss. *First in His Class: The Bill Clinton Biography.* New York: Touchstone Books, 1995, p. 251.

Page 20, line 20: Jerry Oppenheimer. *State of a Union: Inside the Complex Marriage of Bill and Hillary Clinton.* New York: HarperCollins, 2000, p. 70.

Page 24, line 17: *Living History*, p. 41

Page 24, line 21: Ibid., p. 42.

Chapter 3

Page 28, line 8: Gail Sheehy. *Hillary's Choice.* New York: Random House, 1999, p. 86.

Page 29, line 7: *Living History*, p. 52.

Page 30, line 17: Ibid., p. 64.

Page 31, line 2: *State of a Union*, p. 116.

Page 33, line 3: *Living History*, p. 66.

Page 35, lines 17 and 18: *Hillary's Choice*, p. 121.

Chapter 4

Page 39, line 12: Roger Morris. *Partners in Power: The Clintons and Their America.* New York: Henry Holt and Company, 1996, p. 225.

Page 40, line 11: *Living History*, p. 85.

Page 43, line 7: *Hillary's Choice*, p. 147.

Page 47, line 15: *Living History*, p. 100.

Chapter 5

Page 49, line 8: Ibid., p. 103.

Page 51, lines 1 and 3: Ibid., p. 109.

Page 52, line 5: Ibid., p. 110.

Page 52, line 14: Ibid., p. 105.

Page 55, line 4: Ibid., p. 125.

Chapter 6

Page 57, line 7: *Hillary's Choice*, p. 219.

Page 58, line 24: Michael Kramer. "The Political Interest." *Time.* 31 Jan. 1994. 26 Oct. 2007. www.time.com/time/magazine/article/0,9171,980052,00.html

Page 60, line 18: *Living History*, p. 194.

Page 62, line 10: Ibid., p. 303.

Page 62, line 17: Hillary Rodham Clinton. "Speech at the United Nations Fourth World Conference on Women, Beijing, China." 5 Sept. 1995. 26 Oct. 2007. http://clinton4.nara.gov/WH/EOP/First_Lady/html/generalspeeches/1995/plenary.html

Page 63, line 3: Bill Clinton. *My Life.* New York: Alfred A. Knopf, 2004, p. 671.

Chapter 7

Page 72, line 6: *Hillary's Choice*, p. 328.

Chapter 8

Page 77, line 27: Ibid., p. 502.

Page 79, lines 20 and 21: "Hillary Confirms Senate Campaign." BBC News. 7 Feb. 2000. 26 Oct. 2007. http://news.bbc.co.uk/1/hi/world/americas/632645.stm

Page 81, line 5: Michael Ellison. "How Hillary Vanquished Lazio." *The Guardian.* 8 Nov. 2000. 26 Oct. 2007. www.guardian.co.uk/US_election_race/Story/0,2763,394348,00.html

Page 81, line 24: *Living History*, p. 528.

Chapter 9

Page 84, line 7: Senator Hillary Rodham Clinton. "Statement On The Floor of the United States Senate in Response to the World Trade Center and Pentagon Attacks." Senator Hillary Clinton Web site. 12 Sept. 2001. 26 Oct. 2006. http://clinton.senate.gov/~clinton/news/2001/09/2001912D06.html

Page 86, line 4: Robert Kurson. "Hillary's Last Chance." *Esquire.* October 2003, p. 184.

Page 87, line 25: Elizabeth Kolbert. "The Student." *The New Yorker.* October 13, 2004, p. 65.

Page 90, line 7: "Senator Clinton Calls for New American Consensus to Meet Foreign Policy Challenges." United States Senate. 31 Oct. 2006. 26 Oct. 2007. www.senate.gov/~clinton/news/statements/record.cfm?id=265805

Page 91, line 6: Hillary Clinton. "Special Feature." HillaryClinton.com 26 Oct. 2007. www.hillaryclinton.com/feature/in/

Page 91, line 20: "Hillary on Iraq." OpinionJournal. 8 Feb. 2007. 26 Oct. 2007. www.opinionjournal.com/editorial/feature.html?id=110009637

Page 93, line 6: "Hillary Clinton Is 'in' Iowa." RadioIowa. 27 Jan. 2007. 26 Oct. 2007. http://learfield.typepad.com/radioiowa/2007/01/hillary_clinton.html

Page 95, line 5: Hillary Clinton. "Economic Policy: Modern Progressive Vision: Shared Prosperity" HillaryClinton.com 29 May 2007. 26 Oct. 2007. www.hillaryclinton.com/news/speech/view/?id=1839

Select Bibliography

Bernstein, Carl. *A Woman in Charge.* New York: Knopf Publishing Group, 2007.

Clinton, Bill. *My Life.* New York: Alfred A. Knopf, 2004.

Clinton, Hillary Rodham. *An Invitation to the White House: At Home with History.* New York: Simon and Schuster, 2000.

Clinton, Hillary Rodham. *It Takes a Village and Other Lessons Children Teach Us.* New York: Simon and Schuster, 1996.

Clinton, Hillary Rodham. *Living History.* New York: Simon and Schuster, 2003.

Clinton, Hillary Rodham. Speech at the United Nations Fourth World Conference on Women, Beijing, China. 5 Sept. 1995. http://clinton4.nara.gov/WH/EOP/First_Lady/html/generalspeeches/1995/plenary.html

"The Clinton Years." Frontline. http://www.pbs.org/wgbh/pages/frontline/shows/clinton/cron

"It's Official: Hillary Clinton Announces Senate Candidacy." *CNN.com.* http://archives.cnn.com/2000/ALLPOLITICS/stories/02/06/hillary.announce.01/index.html

Kolbert, Elizabeth. "The Student." *The New Yorker.* 13 October 2004.

Kurson, Robert. "Hillary's Last Chance." *Esquire.* October 2003, p. 184.

Maraniss, David. *First in His Class: The Biography of Bill Clinton.* New York: Touchstone, 1995.

Milton, Joyce. *The First Partner: Hillary Rodham Clinton.* New York: William Morrow and Company, 1999.

Oppenheimer, Jerry. *State of a Union: Inside the Complex Marriage of Bill and Hillary Clinton.* New York: HarperCollins, 2000.

Sheehy, Gail. *Hillary's Choice.* New York: Random House, 1999.

Michael Burgan is a freelance writer for children and adults. A history graduate of the University of Connecticut, he has written more than 100 fiction and nonfiction children's books for various publishers. For adult audiences, he has written news articles, essays, and plays. Michael Burgan is a recipient of an Educational Press Association of America award and belongs to the Society of Children's Book Writers and Illustrators.

Image Credits

Time & Life Pictures/Getty Images, cover (top), 4–5, 11; Najlah Feanny/Corbis Saba, cover (bottom), 2, 82, 101 (top right); Doug Kanter/AFP/Getty Images, 8, 100 (top); Syed Jan Sabawoon/epa/Corbis, 13; Brooks Kraft/Sygma/Corbis, 14, 23, 25, 31, 96 (top, all); Tim Boyle/Getty Images, 16, 21; AP Photo, 19; Wally McNamee/Corbis, 26; Cynthia Johnson/Time Life Pictures/Getty Images, 28; David Hume Kennerly/Getty Images, 32, 97 (top); Mike Stewart/Corbis Sygma, 37, 38, 42, 44, 98 (top left); AP Photo/Donald R. Broyles, 41, 98 (top right); AP Photo/Ron Edmonds, 46; Library of Congress, photograph courtesy of The White House, 48, 55, 99 (top); Steve Liss/Time Life Pictures/Getty Images, 51; Brad Markel/Liaison Agency/Getty Images, 53; AP Photo/Denis Paquin, 56; Diana Walker/Time Life Pictures/Getty Images, 59; Stephen Jaffe/Getty Images, 61; Attar Maher/Corbis Sygma, 63; Vince Bucci/AFP/Getty Images, 65; Ron Sachs/CNP/Corbis, 66, 72; AP Photo/Doug Mills, 69; Jason Szenes/Corbis Sygma, 70; AP Photo/Ron Frehm, 74; Don Emmert/AFP/Getty Images, 76; Susan Stava/Sygma/Corbis, 78; Chris Hondros/Newsmakers/Getty Images, 80; Spencer Platt/Getty Images, 84; Scott Barbour/Getty Images, 86, 101 (top left); Luke Frazza/AFP/Getty Images, 88; Dusan Vranic/AFP/Getty Images, 90; Tannen Maury/epa/Corbis, 92; Steve Pope/epa/Corbis, 94; Corel, 96 (bottom left); NASA, 96 (bottom right), 99 (bottom left), 101 (bottom); Courtesy Intel Museum Archives and Collections, 97 (bottom left); Photodisc, 97 (bottom right); Keystone/Getty Images, 98 (bottom); Scott Peterson/Liaison/Getty Images, 99 (bottom right); Getty Images, 100 (bottom left); Digital Vision, 100 (bottom right).